The Employee Entrepreneur's Guide to Starting and Incorporating a Side Business

Eric Thomas

Printed in the United States of America

First Printing, 2014

ISBN: 0615911544
ISBN: 978-0-615-91154-0

www.theDiverseMind.com

This book is also available in digital format.

Cover by Hermann Joubert
Copy editing by Kerrie McLoughlin

To Pat, for supporting me and resurrecting me with your love.

To my children, follow your dreams as consistently as day follows night.

CONTENTS

INTRODUCTION

THE STORY OF DAVID

Dana sticks her head out of the bedroom door and peers down the hallway. She steps out and walks down the stairs, carrying their son and guiding their daughter. She glances at her husband David, who is sitting stoically on the sofa. She walks into the kitchen and lifts a set of keys from the hook beside the door that leads to the garage, looks over her left shoulder and says, "I'm going out for milk." She pauses, draws in a deep breath, then adds, "and to see dad." A flash of anger rushes through David. The vibration from the garage door ceases, confirming that he is alone. He relaxes as the sofa embraces his tired, drained body. Just as his body begins to appreciate the comfort of the position, he leans forward and rises from the sofa. He moves with an

1

unconscious ease into the kitchen and lifts the remaining set of keys from the hook beside the door that leads to the garage. He slides into his truck. The warm, soft leather seats welcome him. For a moment, the somberness on his face is escorted away by a prideful smile. He loves this truck. It serves as his reward, his trophy for graduating college, for putting in the long hours and hard work that led to his promotion last year. He looks in the rear view mirror to confirm that the garage doors are closed, then nods to himself that all the windows in the truck are down.

He tilts his head back, closes his eyes and asks his thoughts to take him away to a time of promise, happiness, and bright futures. It's 2003 and the 94-degree temperature is a harbinger that summer isn't going to stand behind spring much longer. He fondly remembers walking ecstatically across the stage, offering his right hand to the school president and his left hand clutching something that no one in his family had ever held, a college degree. In this moment of solitude David engages in a conversation with himself. *I followed the road map that everyone said would lead to success and happiness. I made good decisions, worked hard, graduated college, got a good job, got married, and had kids. I did everything right, so how could my life turn out this way? Why can't I find a job?* The stress is suffocating him. He raises the key to slide it into the ignition. He thinks of his son and his daughter. He thinks of his wife. He can still feel the sting from her last words, "and to see dad." He slides the key into the ignition and with an effortless twist of his right wrist; David has found a solution to his problem.

David was downsized, laid off, or, as it was put to him by his manager, "the fat that needed to be trimmed." The number one goal of a business is to make a profit. No profit, no business. To achieve this goal businesses aggressively seek tools and processes that will make the business more efficient and profitable. Technology and a global economy are the adversaries of the employee today. Every day brings the possibility that you will lose your job to a new computer program or to someone overseas who can do your job for half the cost. Since business is always in pursuit of making a profit, you are always an option to be cut. Nearly every piece of financial advice spoken or written will tell you to save money for an emergency fund. This is sound advice, but I don't believe it is enough. Times have changed drastically, and the financial advice has not kept up with the times.

For the average individual or family the primary expenses are rent/mortgage, groceries, car payment, car insurance, gasoline, cell phone and utilities (water, electricity, heat). There are many more expenses that could be listed, but I want to stick with the items that are necessary. For a single person, these monthly expenses will average $1,900. For a family, the average is $5,000 per month. These numbers will certainly differ according to where you live, but they work fine for this conversation. The prevailing financial advice is that your emergency fund should carry you for six months in the event of job loss. In today's climate, however, I would suggest a year of funding is needed. More people are looking for fewer jobs, and it's not unusual for a person to be out of work for a year. Under these circumstances, a single person would need approximately $11,400 dollars, and a family would need $30,000 dollars to cover living expenses for six months. A year would require $22,800 for a single person and $60,000 for a family. With nearly 30 percent of Americans not having any monetary cushion, it is very likely that you don't have this kind of money put aside or know anyone who does. It is very difficult to save these amounts, and very few people have the capacity to do so.

Saving money for lean times is an option, but alone is not a very good option. It is a reactive approach to a situation where you need to be proactive. Savings is the mindset of a consumer. You need to be a producer. You need to produce income the same as a farmer plants a seed in the ground and produces a crop. The farmer never worries about how he is going to eat because he knows how to produce food. You must have that same mindset. Once you know how to produce income, you will no longer live under the fear and anxiety of being fired or laid off from a job.

This book is about showing you how to be a producer like the farmer, but instead of producing food you produce income; an income that is generated by a business that you created from an idea that you have or a hobby. If you're looking for some grand plan that will turn you into a millionaire overnight, I suggest you put this book down and invest your time in one of the many "get rich quick ideas" that are so prevalent on the Internet. I don't have any "get rich quick" ideas to share, but I can show you how to start a business that will support you in the lean times, allow you to maintain your current job, and give you the opportunity to eventually leave the workforce and become a full-time entrepreneur. Let me share those things with you.

CHAPTER ONE

THE EVOLUTION OF THE EMPLOYEE ENTREPRENEUR

The Way It Was

The business world has consisted of two roles: the employee and the entrepreneur. The current business model bears no semblance to its former self. The business model that prevailed just a few decades ago provided a level of comfort and stability to the workforce. The foundation of that model was the individual. Companies would hire an individual and invest resources into that individual, and that individual would in turn invest himself or herself into the company. Then the individual, along with the company, would grow and prosper.

That model is gone, and it has been replaced by an unpredictable model where each day a new technology affords companies the opportunity to increase profits and decrease costs by outsourcing and eliminating jobs, and therefore eliminate the individual. This daily opportunity to outsource and eliminate jobs, a slow economy, rising prices on nearly all essential items, and a consistently present potential to be laid off has made the employee uncomfortable. As a result a third category has evolved, the Employee Entrepreneur.

The Way It Is

Fate had other plans for David. His truck ran out of gas while idling in the garage that evening. One week later, he was offered a job at the bank. David works as a bank teller, but he discovered a passion for gardening. Friends and people in the community are always asking David for vegetables from his garden, and he is always happy to share the bounty from his harvest. Driving home one afternoon David realized that families want to save money and eat healthy but they don't have a lot of free time. These families also have enough backyard space to hold a small garden. David is about to implement a key principle in the creation of a business: finding a need and filling it. David starts his gardening business by using some of his savings to buy a commercial grade tiller, a variety of seed, and some fertilizer. He passes out flyers around town, and within a month he lands his first client.

The spring season is approaching, and his gardening business is growing faster than a Nebraska corn-stalk. David works at the bank during the day and takes care of his gardening customers in the evenings and on weekends. David has doubled his income. He earns a salary from his job at the bank, and his gardening business is generating revenue nearly equivalent to his salary. Who said you can't have your cake and eat it too? David has accomplished something much more substantial than the doubling of his income; he has recovered his power of self-determination.

Become the Tiger

You have utility bills, probably a mortgage, car payments, credit cards, student loans and, most importantly, children. Like many employees, you probably feel trapped in your job. The job market is in disarray and the economy is sluggish. Enormous financial responsibilities and the sluggish economy have put you, and many like you, at a serious disadvantage. Your employer knows that good-paying job opportunities are scarce. Your employer also figures that you are overburdened with debt and can't afford to miss a single paycheck. Your employer takes advantage of your predicament and eliminates positions which will increase the company's profits and assign the overflow work to you and your colleagues. This shortens deadlines, increases stress, and requires you to work beyond normal business hours, and - in some cases - weekends. Your power of self-determination is slowly being transferred to the employer. The relationship between an animal and a trainer is a good way to illustrate how this power can be regained.

A trainer has a tiger perform a trick and, if done correctly, the tiger is rewarded with a snack treat. Let's suppose that one day the taste buds of the tiger change, and now the tiger doesn't like the snack treat anymore. Because the tiger no longer desires the snack treat, those snack treats no longer carry sufficient influence to move the tiger to do the tricks. The tiger has found a freedom, and the trainer will have to find another method of influence, or lose his ability to manipulate the tiger. When you create a business, you create a freedom. When your business produces enough revenue to support your lifestyle, then the trainer, - your manager/boss, - can no longer use the snack treat (the fear of losing your job) to manipulate you. You will no longer feel pressured to perform difficult tasks, work beyond normal business hours, work on weekends, or tolerate harassment. You will have become the tiger that is no longer influenced by the snack treat. You will have become the tiger that is free.

CHAPTER TWO

BECOMING AN EMPLOYEE ENTREPRENEUR

What is an Entrepreneur?

The dictionary defines an entrepreneur as "a person who organizes and manages any enterprise, especially a business, usually with considerable initiative and risk." I prefer a simpler, broader definition. An entrepreneur is anyone who creates an opportunity by putting together ideas, people or resources to manifest a primary idea. Entrepreneurs are all around you. Entrepreneurs are on your job, in your church, in your classroom, at your gym. There's an entrepreneur in every home, even in your home. Take a moment and introduce yourself to the entrepreneur in your home the next time you look in the mirror.

Benefits of Entrepreneurship

Freedom - The day I decided to try my hand at entrepreneurship I immediately reaped what is for me its primary benefit: freedom. My business had not generated a single dime, but I felt a freedom that I had never experienced. No longer would my financial fate be tied to the whims of a fickle boss or a slow economy. My income would no longer be dictated by company growth, the state of the economy or the yearly "cost of living" raise. The decision to become an entrepreneur was a decision to take control of my livelihood.

Peace of mind - The fear of being laid off or fired is an enormous and influential fear. This is a very real fear for many in the workplace, and it may be for you as well, but you don't have to live with this fear. Becoming an entrepreneur will lessen or entirely remove this fear because you are building a safety net for you and your family, a safety net that will bring you peace of mind.

Added Value - To be an entrepreneur your mindset must change from that of a consumer (employee) to a producer (owner). Employees have little to concern themselves with other than their next project/assignment and playing nice with their co-workers.

Entrepreneurship requires you to think broadly, and long term, far beyond your next paycheck. You will have a different perspective and will begin to understand why your owners/managers make some of the decisions they make. Your new perspective will prepare you for how management is thinking and you won't be surprised, like your colleagues are, when acquisitions take place or when measures are implemented to cut costs.

What is a Business?

A business is the exchange of goods and/or services. A business does not require a building or an office, nor does it require a product. This may sound odd, but money is not a requirement for a business. Let's look at David, the bank teller who operated a gardening business on the side. David didn't have a building or an office - he was mobile. He didn't have a product - he provided a service. David did use money, but he could have chosen to barter as a method of compensation instead of money.

Now that you know what constitutes a business you should also understand business itself. It doesn't matter if you plan to run a business or to be an employee; you will participate in business. Understanding business will teach you about taxes, cash flow, credit, how to protect your assets and how to spot growth opportunities. An individual and a business are very much alike. The individual must be marketed to gain employment, and a business must market to get customers. The individual must have income, and a business must have earnings. An individual has bills that must be paid, and a business has expenses and expenditures. The more you know about business the more likely it is that you will be successful in life.

Side Business Model

Everyone goes into business to make money, but a side business has to do more than just make money. I have three criteria for creating a side business. Your side business should:

1. Have the capacity to create enough income so you can leave your job, if you decide to do so.

2. Generate free time so you can enjoy your family, experience travel, and explore the other interests in your life. It makes no sense to start a business where you spend as much or more time involved in your business as you did with your job. You would basically have traded one job for another, and that is not the result you want.

3. Coexist with your full-time job. You don't want your side business to have more than a minimal interference with your full-time job. It is your full-time job that will support you until your business becomes profitable.

I have put together a list to help you filter out business ideas that don't meet the three criteria for creating a side business.

• You and/or your immediate family should be able to manage the business.

• It's important to start a side business doing something you enjoy.

• You should be able to train others to perform your role in the business; otherwise you're chained to the business because you're the only person with the know-how.

• Avoid brick and mortar businesses. They require a large initial investment to get started. They require a lot of resources to grow and maintain. They will keep you chained to the business until you can afford to hire someone to replace you.

• Outsource. I devote an entire chapter to this topic. Use independent contractors and avoid hiring employees. The taxes, (FICA, unemployment, payroll) accounting, insurance, federal guidelines and mandates that come along with employees equal one massive headache.

• At least 30% of the business should be able to be managed via the internet. This will significantly reduce the time you spend on manual tasks within your business and free you up to do more important things like travel and spend time with your family.

Sacrifice

My son and daughter would run into the room under the spell of excitement, bursting to tell me about a new idea that was consuming their thoughts. I would listen intently, make a few comments, and as they were leaving the room I would say, "There's no success without sacrifice." In an instant, their demeanors would change, their shoulders would sag, and their excitement would exit as quickly as it had arrived. On a few occasions they would come back to me a little less excited but more serious and full of questions. Their return told me that they were serious and willing to sacrifice. Your excitement will wane, and you will be faced with the reality of sacrificing. You may have to give up watching your favorite TV shows, sleep less, spend less time with the family, divert most or all discretionary monies to the business which may mean less shopping, bringing your own lunch to work or take fewer vacations. Everyone has ideas, but only with sacrifice will you see your ideas manifested.

You Need a Plan

World War II Army General George S. Patton said, "A good plan today is better than a perfect plan tomorrow." General George S. Patton may have been referring to plans in a broad manner, but I think his quote can be directly applied to business plans.

In my opinion, having a business plan is a requirement and, as General George S. Patton suggests, it does not have to be perfect. Unfortunately, too many entrepreneurs get bogged down in creating the perfect business plan. Remember, this is a side business, and developing a full-blown business plan would be extreme, so keep it simple. I understand that you have big plans for your side business -and that is wonderful - but for now just put together a good business plan. As your business grows and you see the need for a loan or investors, that would be when you should invest the time and money to put together the perfect, full-blown business plan.

Honestly, if your business grows to the point where you need investors, you may not need a business plan because you would have demonstrated the most important facet of a business plan, which is that there is a demand for your products or services.

Is It Safe?

Business owners are not aware of how their business is being stifled by not using the internet. I am often surprised to hear the high level of concern from people in general, but especially from entrepreneurs, about the safety of sending and receiving payments across the internet. If you are squeamish about transacting business over the internet, you may want to reassess operating a side business since it is nearly impossible to operate any business without involving the internet.

The year is 1995, and I am in the grocery store about to purchase groceries using a paper check. The clerk gives me the total and I whip out my checkbook along with my drivers license, for identification. I give the check and drivers license to the clerk. The check contains my bank account number, routing number, name, address and phone number, and my drivers license number is my social security number. Essentially I have given the clerk everything needed to create another me. When you really think about it, if my information was misused could I really claim identity theft? I had freely given the clerk all the information.

Today, daily transactions are handled much differently. The act of writing a check is going the way of the dinosaur, replaced by the swipe of a plastic card. Personal information is closely guarded, and any organization or person asking for personal information is looked at with a wary eye. The information used to make a purchase online is encrypted by an extremely complex algorithm that would require a supercomputer to decipher. If you look at this from the perspective of identity thieves, it is not worth their effort to spend several days or weeks trying to break into your accounts, which may or may not contain a worthwhile amount of money. It is more lucrative for them to spend several weeks hacking into a database containing thousands of names and passwords that has the potential to expose them to millions of dollars. When transacting business on the internet, use common sense; make purchases and transactions with reputable websites and companies. Using a third party like PayPal when receiving payments from your customers is a real safeguard that protects you and your customer. These simple steps will expand your business opportunities, your revenue and give you peace of mind.

CHAPTER THREE

BUSINESS PRINCIPLES AND IDEAS

"What kind of business should I start?" is the one question that I am asked the most. I won't begin to tell you what business you should go into, but there are methods I use to inspire ideas for a new business, and principles to ensure those ideas will prosper me.

When I was 14 a friend got me a job at the pet store where he worked. The store was owned by two brothers, Jerry and Don. Several times a month, Don would come into the store firing off ideas that he felt would grow the business. Jerry would listen. They would start talking. Talking would lead to arguing. The arguing would simmer until the expletives were added and bring things to a full boil. Occasionally one or the both of them would have to be restrained. This was pure entertainment for me. I would peer between the stacked cans of Alpo dog food on the shelves and watch the fireworks. I often wondered how these guys could go at each other with such ferocity yet continue to work together. And not just work together; they were very successful. They owned eight stores in the area and were adding more. Time passed and the yelling, swearing, and fighting didn't command my attention anymore. I no longer ran to peer between the stacked cans of Alpo dog food on the shelves. Eventually it all became a kind of background noise, but in this noise was Jerry's voice stating three distinct, consistent principles. The brothers attributed their success to these three principles. They constantly argued, but these principles would always guide them to a mutual agreement. These principles continue to guide me in selecting which business idea is best suited for me.

"Everything Ain't for Everybody"

A co-worker named Susan shared with me that she always wanted to open a restaurant, and now was the time to make it happen. She was going to open a restaurant in the space below our office. I told her it was an excellent idea for someone else, but a terrible idea for her. The only thing that Susan knew about restaurants was that they sold food. I watched Susan struggle daily with her restaurant. She was losing money every day, and the restaurant never reached profitability. The restaurant closed six months after opening.

Susan failed because she ignored the principle that *everything isn't for everybody*. Many business owners ignore this principle and fail similarly. Just because you have an idea or a desire doesn't mean you are the person best suited to manifest that idea or desire.

Do What You Know

What is your answer to the question, I know-how to ____? When I ask people this question their answer almost always involves what they do for a living. You may be exercising your know-how on your full-time job. If you are already exercising your know-how, why not take the same skills that you are using on your full-time job and apply them to create a side business?

Dennis was very successful at applying his know-how to start his side business. Dennis is a registered nurse who works at the hospital as a nursing instructor. He teaches nurses who work in the high-stress trauma units how to manage that stress. Dennis found out that only his hospital offered this type of training and decided to offer this service to nurses in the surrounding areas. He placed a small ad in the local newspaper and used his doctor and nurse friends to help spread the word about his business. Within a few weeks Dennis had rented a small conference room at the library and began teaching his specialized stress management classes to area nurses.

Do What you Love

Susan didn't give up after the restaurant failed. She picked herself up and opened another business, but this time she used her passion and know-how as guides. Susan loves cars and is extremely knowledgeable about cars. She knows more about cars than most men do. Prior to Susan opening the restaurant, I suggested she become an automobile consultant for women. When it comes to auto repair, women are more likely to be advised to have automobile repairs done that aren't needed and charged more for auto repairs. Susan is a perfect solution to these problems. She diagnoses the problem and provides the customer a detailed output of the problem and an estimate of the repair cost. Susan saves her clients hundreds, and in some case thousands, of dollars in unnecessary repair work and inflated repair costs.

The principles of do what you know, do what you love and "everything ain't for everybody" were the foundation of Jerry and

Don's pet store chain and the other businesses they created over the years. Dennis and Susan implemented their passion and know-how in the creation of their business. Susan came to understand that "everything ain't for everybody" after her failed attempt at being a restaurateur. It is your passion that will move you through the difficult times when you want to quit and your know-how will reduce the mistakes that everyone makes when starting a business. Now, I'm not telling you that you should only start a business doing something that you know, but starting a business in an area where you have experience and knowledge really increases your opportunity for success. Starting a business in an area that is foreign to you gives your competition significant advantages over you. Your precious money and time will go to learning the specifics of that business and overcoming mistakes while your competition spends their money on attracting new customers and improving their product or service.

Add the Difference

Ideas for a business are in your space all the time. Very few businesses spring up because of some new, grand idea. Most new businesses are created based on improving an existing product or service. There are at least eight fast food restaurants where the hamburger is the featured item on the menu. How can so many restaurants thrive selling the same item? By taking an existing product and adding something different, that's how. I call it *adding the difference*. Burger King and McDonald's are excellent examples of this philosophy. Burger King added two differences. They "flame broil" their burgers and give the customer the opportunity to "have it your way." These companies took an existing product, the hamburger, added a difference and formed new businesses. Pay attention to the products and services that you use. Ask yourself what difference you would add to that product or service. Your answer could inspire a new business.

Complaints Equal Opportunity

People complain when they are dissatisfied. Being able to ease or eliminate that dissatisfaction is an opportunity for a new business. For years cell phone users complained about being required to sign long-term service contracts with cell phone carriers. That dissatisfaction was the seed for the prepaid cell phone industry.

People also complain when a product or service isn't available in the marketplace. Not too long ago I lived in a community where there was no grocery store. The nearest store was more than 10 miles away. Community members complained, and now there are three grocery stores where there were none.

In every complaint there is potential for a new business. The next time you hear someone complaining, don't walk away. They may be giving you the business idea that will make you millions.

Just Listen

My son plays soccer for his high school. One evening I was sitting in the bleachers watching him play. Seated behind me were two parents with children on the opposing team. Like many parents, they feel that their children have the skills to garner an athletic scholarship. In college soccer the coaches don't have the time or the budget to travel to each high school to scout a player, so the player has to find a method of generating interest from coaches. In essence, the player recruits the coach. Hopefully the coach will see potential and recruit the player. I had solved this same problem for my son a few months earlier.

As I listened to these parents, an idea for a business began to develop. I could re-purpose the idea that I had used for my son and offer it as a service to parents of high school children interested in obtaining scholarships for soccer. Over the next several days I devised a pricing plan, created a company name, put up a website, and ordered business cards. In the span of two weeks I was ready for customers. Sometimes you only need to be quiet and listen to get a great business idea.

Some of My Ideas

Here are some business ideas that I have come up with and some that I know are in operation. These ideas aren't intrusive; they co-exist well with a full-time work schedule.

Online Teacher/Tutor – You don't need much to get started. A webcam, hi-speed internet connection, phone, computer and a headset is about all the equipment you will need. There are several inexpensive and free online whiteboard options that can serve as your blackboard. There's no travel time or expense. You can do the work from anywhere and make your own schedule.

Online Store – A co-worker and good friend started an online toy store. He found several reputable global trade companies online that he used to purchase products at a discount. He invested in an e-commerce website, a logo, some online advertising dollars, and a lot of time. In the span of two years his company has grown and generates over $150,000 in revenue per year. Aside from the extra income, the best part about this is he still works full-time. He doesn't sacrifice performance at work and he only spends an average of 10 hours a week managing his business. His book *The Profit Principle* by G.R. Massey shows you step by step how to start an online store.

Farmer/Gardener – I know you're probably scratching your head about this business idea, but hear me out. It's not for everyone, but it is a viable option for many and maybe even for you. I'm in no way suggesting that you buy a few hundred acres and some farm equipment and start farming, because that won't fit the Employee/Entrepreneur model. I'm talking about starting small farms in your community. People everywhere know about the economic and health benefits of growing their own food, but they don't have the time or the know-how to get it done. Many homes have backyards that are big enough to support a garden, and some communities have unused land. All you need is a small tiller (avg. $500 new), fertilizer, some seeds, and a few other inexpensive accessories to get started.

An explanation of your service to a potential customer may involve the following: Assess the garden site; prepare the client's soil and plant the seeds; and give your client some points on daily maintenance and things they need to be aware of to keep the vegetables growing. You can offer various packages to fit customer needs. These can include contacting the client via e-mail weekly for status updates and online meetings to give information and answer questions. Provide limited site visits to assess the crop. This can be a seasonal or year-round business that can grow food for people in your community and money for you.

Application Developer – Creating applications for the iPhone or Android market is very profitable, and the consumer demand for these applications is insatiable. All you need to get started is a computer, an internet connection, and some programming software (downloadable from the internet). Here are some of the benefits of developing applications:

- No formal training required.

- Most tools are downloadable from the internet for free.

- Hundreds of free online tutorials and videos.

- Marketplace for applications is open and non-restrictive.

- Build it. Market it. Transfer the money into your account.

- You can work wherever there is a computer.

- The opportunity is available to anyone. There are kids as young as 12 who have created applications that are in the marketplace generating income.

•Only maintenance is needed once the application is developed and in the marketplace.

This is an opportunity with a great deal of flexibility and advantages.

Consultant – Have you been cited for awards at your company? Are you the person others come to see when they want to learn how to "do it right"? Are you often asked "what's your secret" or "how did you get so good at…"? All of these questions indicate that you are good at what you do. You have the makings of a consultant.

Expertise in any field or industry can be leveraged in the creation of a business. Becoming a consultant takes very little to get started. A professionally designed website, business cards, and some time is about all you need to get started. The same people that asked "what's your secret" or "how did you get so good at…" can be your first clients.

Sports Photographer – Most high schools have a dedicated photographer for the football team because it is usually the high-profile sport at the school. Sports like volleyball, track, baseball, and soccer are typically ignored. Quality digital sports pictures are an expected component of a player's profile, and they are vital in garnering interest from college coaches. Be aware that people are sensitive to a stranger taking pictures of their children. You will be easier to accept if you have a child in high school or you have an existing relationship with a school. If you don't have these relationships, I suggest you attend the parent meetings associated with the sport and offer your services.

One way to get started is to attend a few games and take some pictures. Post the pictures on a photo-sharing website in an account that is secure and owned by you. Smugmug.com or a similar site will have what you need. Tell the parents where you have the pictures hosted and let them see your work. Most good photo-sharing sites will allow you to set a price for your photos and allow them to be purchased. A high-quality digital camera and a little photography experience can make sports photography a nice side business for you.

Don't Be So Anxious to Leave

One afternoon as I was leaving the computer store I ran into James, a former co-worker. He looked distraught and had lost a lot of weight. The last memory I had of James was him happily walking into his manager's office. As he walked into the office I recalled a phrase I had developed to express when I am disappointed with a choice made by my children, "I thought you were smarter than that decision." James cleared his throat and began to tell me what had transpired in his life since I had last seen him.

James was the technology buyer for our company. He earned a six-figure salary but he traveled a lot, and the volatile relationship he had with his manager was a constant source of frustration and anxiety. I suggested he move to another department but James had other plans. James decided to leave the company and form a consulting business. He would advise small businesses concerning large technology purchases and investments. There were a few companies that had assured James they could use his services, and with his work ethic he would certainly get more customers soon. Tuesday afternoon James proudly walked into the office of his manager and presented him with a letter of resignation. Two weeks later and James was on his own.

James immediately contacted those potential clients, only to discover they wouldn't need his services until the next year or later. The next six months he spent marketing his company and diligently seeking customers. With no source of income, his savings were quickly disappearing. In the span of nine months James had used virtually all of his savings, closed his business, and was in desperate need of a job. James is an example of allowing emotion to dictate decisions. James should have tried to reconcile with his manager or move to another department to reduce the frustration and anxiety. James took the promise of customers as a guarantee that he would have customers.

I passed along some words of encouragement and wished him well. Here are a few reasons why you don't need to be in a hurry to leave your job.

Failure Rate - 50% of all businesses fail in the first few years. Poor timing, poor planning, lack of capital, and technical innovations are just a few factors that contribute to the early demise of a business. With only a 50% success rate it makes a lot of sense to stay employed and continue that steady income stream so you can maintain your lifestyle. Growing a business takes time, and leaving your job will put the pressure on you and your business to replace the income that was previously provided by your job. Staying on your job will keep you from making rash decisions in the effort to grow your business and minimize the pressure of your business having to instantly succeed.

Insurance & Benefits - Do you know how much it costs to insure a family of four? On the average it cost between $400-$800 dollars per month for health insurance for a family of four. And there's still dental and vision insurance to consider. You could be looking at a $1,000 per month just in insurance expenses. Can your new business cover this cost? Probably not, and this is another reason why remaining employed is a good idea. Your employer is paying at least 50% of your insurance costs, and many companies offer a 401(k) retirement plan where your dollar investment in the plan is matched anywhere from 25% to 100%. You also need to consider sick time, vacation time, and holiday time off. Insurance, paid time off and retirement are very good incentives for keeping your job.

Personal Gratification - A job does more than generate money. Jobs have a social benefit attached, along with delivering a feeling of accomplishment. What would you do if you didn't have to go to work? What about the relationships that have grown over the years with your colleagues? What about the pride and accomplishment you feel when you see an idea manifested or in closing a big deal? There are a lot of things to consider before walking away from your job. Be patient and think carefully.

CHAPTER FOUR

TOOLS FOR YOUR TOOLBOX

Patty has been in business for eight years. She is the owner of a very successful afterschool program for elementary school children with an enrollment of over 100 children. Every Monday, Wednesday, and Friday evening, Patty drives to the school and spends about an hour collecting payments from the parents. The parents pay by check. Patty goes home, opens her spreadsheet, and types the payment amount beside the name of each child for that week. She then writes the amount of each check onto the bank deposit slip and totals all the checks. The last step is driving to the bank the following morning to deposit the checks. This is a manual process and there are several opportunities for errors, like the incorrect totaling of the bank deposit or losing a check.

Patty is only working 30 hours a week and this process is only consuming 10 of those hours a week. Wouldn't those 10 hours be better utilized if they were spent improving the experience of the children in the program, training the staff, having a brainstorming session, or just having more time to enjoy life? Redundant, manual work can be nearly eliminated if you have the right tools in your toolbox. Patty can use one of the many easy and inexpensive online or onsite payment tools that would enable the parents to use their debit or credit cards. An online or onsite payment tool would eliminate the inefficient process of collecting, posting, and depositing payments and would return 10 hours of time to her.

When you think of tools you think of a hammer, wrench, or screwdriver. I also consider a phone, a website, the internet, and even money as tools. In your business you should consistently look for areas that need improvement. Find the tool that will provide improvement, and put that tool in your toolbox. Use tools that are free or inexpensive whenever possible. In Patty's situation there are several tools available. One payment tool will cost her three cents per parent to use while another will cost 17 cents per parent. Both payment tools work equally well, so the less expensive tool should be implemented. Look for tools to help you personally, as well. If you need to improve in the area of speaking, then join a Toastmasters International chapter or use one of the many apps created to help with public speaking.

When you seek growth your toolbox will grow, and so will your business. Regardless of what kind of business you decide to enter, these tools are great to have in your toolbox.

Privacy

Post Office Box

Post Office boxes (PO box) offer several advantages for entrepreneurs. PO boxes are permanent addresses, whereas a home office address would need to change as you change residences.

PO boxes provide several levels of security. First, using a PO box ensures that your personal address remains unknown to your customers. Additionally, mail delivered to a post office box is kept under lock and key until you retrieve it, unlike many home mailboxes, which are accessible to mail thieves.

Mail is delivered to post office boxes much earlier than mail that is delivered to homes or businesses. It's a real convenience for you to pick up mail on your schedule. Deliveries of packages are always accepted at PO boxes because there is always someone available to sign for the parcel, unlike at a home, where you may be unavailable.

The use of a PO box enables a home-based business to expand into other cities and states without opening satellite offices. PO boxes can be opened in any city that has a post office, and mail can be forwarded from those boxes to the main office location. Your business can grow in other markets without adding office space and additional employees. A visit to USPS.com or to any Post Office location can get you a PO box setup in a few minutes.

Google Voice

Google Voice is an Internet-based service that allows you to give everyone one phone number and forward that number to multiple phones. So, if you switch jobs, change phone services, move, or even go on vacation, your phone number stays the same for people trying to reach you. Google Voice eliminates the problem of having to print new marketing materials because a phone number changes. Put your Google Voice number on all your marketing material and changing cell, home, or business phone numbers won't impact people contacting you.

Google Voice also allows you to screen phone calls, block phone numbers, and apply rules based on the caller. When you receive voicemail messages, Google transcribes the message and can send you an email or text message to let you know about the call. A Google Voice number allows you to determine the access customers and business contacts have to you, and it provides another barrier between your business and personal life.

Money Matters

Bookkeeping

One summer morning as I was waiting to see a bank representative, another bank customer and I started talking. He stated that he had left his job a year ago and started a business, and the business wasn't growing as he expected. I inquired about how much he was spending on advertising and the average of his monthly expenses. I was very puzzled when he answered "I don't know." Too many people in the workplace don't have a grasp of where their paycheck dollars are being spent and they bring that same financial unaccountability when they start their business.

If you can't accurately determine what it costs your business to operate, then your business won't survive. Bookkeeping on some level is a requirement. There are a few software products available that don't require you to be a computer guru/accountant to use them. I prefer web-based services. They offer the most flexibility, and I can access the information from anywhere. LessAccounting.com and QuickBooksonline.com are small business-oriented bookkeeping products. Depending on your needs, the prices range from free to about $25 a month. None of these products require you to invest significant time before you begin using them.

Now, if you want nothing to do with bookkeeping or bookkeeping software, then purchase one of these products and hire a bookkeeper. I use QuickBooksonline.com. It has the same capability as the desktop version. I hired a Certified Public Accountant (CPA) and gave her appropriate permission to my QuickBooks account. She works three hours a week to categorize my expenses, run reports, and advise me on which expenses can help reduce my tax liability. If you decide to hire a bookkeeper and use a web-based accounting product, make sure the product has access restrictions. You may not want to give the person you hired full access to your information. In chapter five I'll explain how you can hire professionals for just a few dollars a day.

Business Checking Account

You want there to be a clear distinction between your personal and business affairs in every area possible. This is especially important in the area of money. Thinking that you can use your personal checking account for your business isn't smart thinking. Bankrate.com is a great place to compare services and fees of various banks. Here are a few to keep in mind when you're looking for a business account.

- Ample transaction allowances (150-200). As your business grows, seek banks that offer unlimited transactions.

- No balance requirement or monthly fees.

- Extra freebies like bank cards with rewards points.

- Online bill pay.

Be responsible with the account and keep it unblemished. Overdrawing the account and building a non-sufficient funds (NSF) history will damage your financial relationship with the bank. You want the bank to be an ally that you can turn to when you need a reference or credit.

Business Credit

Did you know that businesses have a credit history just as you have a personal credit history? There is a direct connection between the growth of a business and the credit worthiness of that business. Establishing credit accounts for your business is a very good idea. It may be difficult to get accepted for a business credit card with no history. One way to build credit is to borrow your own money. Most banks will let you open an account and borrow against your deposit. They usually want a minimum of $500 dollars. You can also apply for a secured credit card. The secured credit card and borrowing against your bank deposit are based on the same concept. Be wary of higher-than-average interest rates on both of these borrowing methods, especially with the secured credit card. Bankrate.com is a good site to compare the variety of secured credit cards on the market.

Use credit only when you have the cash on hand to pay for the purchase or in an emergency. Remember, the goal here isn't to go into debt but to establish a credit history for your business. Once you have some credit accounts you can register with Dun & Bradstreet or Experian, which will record and report on all your business credit transactions. The cost to register ranges from $100 to $150.

PayPal

Millions of dollars are sent and received across the internet everyday to pay for goods and services. I can say with near certainty that you will need to send or receive money across the internet. Online payment services electronically transfer money over the internet, and PayPal is the top online payment service. PayPal serves as a middleman in the internet marketplace.

PayPal and other online payment services function in this manner. You visit a website and see a chair that you want to purchase. The seller doesn't know or trust you, and you don't know or trust the seller. To resolve this issue, when you purchase the chair the money is electronically sent to PayPal, which will hold the payment until you receive the chair. The seller can immediately see that they have a confirmed payment. If you don't receive the chair or the chair isn't as promised, then PayPal will return your money. You and the seller are protected.

There are several PayPal alternatives available. These other online payment options are less expensive but aren't as widely used or accepted as PayPal. Be mindful that new customers may not feel comfortable with a lesser-known payment option.

To send and receive payments through PayPal you will need

an email address and your bank account information. If you have an individual PayPal account you can upgrade to a business account by including your employer identification number (EIN). Obtaining an employer identification number is discussed in chapter six.

Image

"Image is everything," and in the world of business few words ring truer. Companies spend millions of dollars every year defining and protecting their image. As a budding entrepreneur you don't have millions to spend on your image, but here are some simple tools that can make you look like a million dollars.

Business Cards

Do you think your resume could fit onto a 3½ x 2 inch card? Probably not, but in essence your business card is the resume for your business. It should look professional, be easy to read, and help customers remember what product/service you offer. Here are a few suggestions to ensure your business card portrays the correct image.

- Use a logo – Have a professional designer create your business logo.

- Have your card printed on good card stock.

- Make your card readable. Use a font size that can be easily read.

- Don't make a personal statement. This isn't the time to show off what you learned in your artist workshop.

- Use professional printing. I know you can use the home printer, but don't. You can get 250-500 cards printed online for under $25. Vistaprint.com is always offering some kind of business card special.

Logo

A logo is purposed with symbolizing the product or service that you provide. The logo should be vector-based, not pixel-based, so that it is scalable (can scale to any size and retain clarity and sharpness) for use on business cards, letterheads, brochures, your website, and even billboards. If the designer doesn't know the difference or can't design in a vector format, find another designer. Your design package should contain at least three initial designs for you to choose from and at least two revisions. A good design can be had for between $75 and $150. You can Google the term "Logo Design" to find designers.

Email Address

Email is widely known as a method of contact but is less well known as a way to define your business image. Whenever I'm given a business card I look for an email address and the email domain name. I am likely to discard the card if there is no email address or if the email domain name is something like @hotmail.com, @gmail.com or @yahoo.com. Now there's nothing wrong with using these companies for personal email, but I expect a business would have made the small investment of time and money to acquire email credentials that represent the business.

Bob@hotmail.com brings to mind a struggling, one-person operation or a hobby being passed off as a business. Firstname.lastname@thediversemind.com impresses me as a business with staff and resources. All the major web hosting companies offer email as part of their hosting package.

Website

Your website is the most important component of your image. The perception in today's market is that a business without a website isn't a business. Your website is your resume, business card, and company representative all bundled into an online package that's visible to over a billion people 24 hours a day, 365

STARTING AND INCORPORATING A SIDE BUSINESS

days a year.

You can hire someone to build your website, or do it yourself. If you choose to do it yourself there are hundreds of free website templates available for download, or you can use one of the many online website builders. Do not use Adobe Flash based templates and online website builders that use Flash in their design if you want your website to be visible to iPhone and iPad users. Apple products do not and will not support Flash.

The online website builders aren't complex but they do require you to invest some time to learn how they work. I would avoid their free versions. The free versions are very limited in the features offered, the templates are poorly designed, and they force you to have ads on your website. There is no reason for a business to be using the free version. If you can't afford $10 a month, you don't need to be starting a business. Squarespace.com, mediatemple.net, and wix.com are some of the online website builders that are quality, filled with features, and are inexpensive. You can build your site and have them host it for about $10 a month. It can take about an hour to build your website, but realistically expect to invest several hours or a day to develop a professional-looking website.

It really saves time, money, and frustration if you know what you want or have a good concept. To help with design ideas, I suggest you visit the websites of companies that share your area of business or re-visit websites that appeal to you for ideas. Look at the layout of the pages, the font sizes and the colors used on the pages. Take screen captures of the pages you like. If you don't like the entire page, note the specific things that you like on the page. Perform this process on a multitude of websites to gather as many ideas as possible. Keep the ideas that generate strong feelings, and put the others aside. These ideas will help you build your website a lot quicker.

Hiring a person to design your website isn't easy, but you can do it successfully by following these guidelines.

Set a Budget - For a basic three- to four-page website (Home, Services, Contact, and About Us pages) you should not spend more than $300. If you're selling products through your website (ecommerce), or you need special functionality, expect the cost to be more.

Some designers will populate the website with your text and pictures if you have the material ready. This is a simple copy and paste process for the designer, and it shouldn't increase cost. If the material isn't ready you will have to do this yourself. Have this discussion before work begins.

Be Specific - Telling a web designer "I want a website" or "I just want something simple" will guarantee that you're going to waste money, time, and be frustrated. The screen captures that you have of other websites will be extremely helpful in providing the designer with a visual example of what you're seeking as a finished product. The more specific you are, the quicker the website will be completed, and the more satisfied you will be in the end.

Be Selective – Potential candidates should have a portfolio of work. If the candidate doesn't have a portfolio, you should disqualify them as a candidate. Ask questions about websites in their portfolio that resemble your ideas. For example: How long did that take to complete? How much did it cost? What language was used to create the website? Can you explain your process for building that website? The designer should be able to answer your questions in layman's terms. The inability to do so is a red flag. You don't want to begin the process confused; it will only get worse. Asking questions will give you a good sense of the designers' level of expertise, patience, and their ability to communicate.

I don't encourage the hiring of friends or relatives. Money, family, and business matters rarely mix well together. When working together there are too many opportunities for disagreement, which can easily bleed over into the relationship. If you hire an outsider and they don't work out, you can fire them and not have to worry about hurt feelings or damaging a relationship.

Set Milestones - You may be prompted for an upfront payment by the designer. I won't give more than 15% of the total cost upfront unless there are special circumstances. For a basic website, milestones usually don't apply. A basic website is a small project, and the designer can deliver the site in a few days or, at most, a week.

A website possessing a lot of features may take up to a month. For such a project I break the design of the website into chunks with a portion of money paid as each chunk is completed to my satisfaction. For example, the total cost of the website is $800. When the Home page is completed to my satisfaction I will submit a payment of $120 and give permission to proceed with the building of the next page. When the next page is completed to my satisfaction I will submit another payment. This will continue until the website is complete, at which time I will make my final payment. This process requires your oversight and timely input but it ensures that you'll stay within your budget and be satisfied.

Compatibility – Not long ago users would access the internet primarily using one browser, Internet Explorer. Now, users access the internet using several browsers. Make sure your website is cross-platform compatible, meaning it can be viewed using the most widely used internet browsers like Firefox, Google Chrome, Safari, and Internet Explorer. Avoid the use of Flash in the design of your website if you want your website to be visible to iPhone and iPad users. Apple products do not support Flash.

Testing, Testing – Once your website is finished the designer should temporarily host it on the internet and send you a link to the site. Put together some friends or family to act as a test group and send the link to them. Make sure all the functions and buttons work on the site. Note any error messages or pictures/videos that don't appear. The bottom line is making sure that everything works to your satisfaction before you pay.

Website Hosting

Every website is comprised of several files, and these files need to be hosted in order to be seen on the internet. A web hosting company takes all the files for your website and puts them onto the internet. Think of it this way; you have a movie and it's ready for the public, but you can't show the movie because you don't have a theater. So, you contact a theater (hosting company) and tell them you want your movie (website) to be shown (hosted) in their theater. You send them the movie (your website files) and they show the movie (make your website visible on the internet).

As I mentioned earlier, many of the online website builders also provide hosting. You can also build your website with one company and choose a different company for your hosting. GoDaddy.com and hostgator.com are the big names in the hosting arena. Whatever host company you choose, they should provide these minimum services:

- Unlimited disk space and bandwidth

- Unlimited sub Domains, FTP accounts, and email accounts

- 99.9% uptime guarantee

- Programming and database features

- Email features

You can expect to pay from $4-11 dollars per month.

Domain Name

Common domain names are all but extinct. With over a billion websites in existence, your first and second choice for a domain name is probably being used, or someone purchased the name and is holding on to it in hopes of selling it to a company and making a chunk of money. The latter is called cybersquatting or domain squatting.

It will take a creative effort to find a domain that isn't in use. You may have to use .net or .org instead of the preferred .com extension. Registering a .com domain name will cost about $11 dollars. I recommend that you pay a few extra dollars to register your domain name privately. When you register a domain you are required to give your contact information. This information is available publicly on the WHOIS database. You risk exposing your name, address, email, and phone number to spammers and marketing firms.

Hosting companies have a domain search bar on their home page. Just type in your domain name, and you can quickly determine if the domain you want is available.

Productivity

A friend of mine asked me to visit a colleague of his named Howard to discuss some ideas Howard had for starting a new business. I was surprised to find that Howard was technologically disadvantaged. Howard had forgotten that *time is money* and though he was saving a few dollars by not investing in current technology, he was losing time which is the equivalent of losing money.

Speed is what you need

A fast, reliable internet connection is no longer a luxury. It is a requirement that should be categorized as a monthly expenditure, the same as your electric bill. There are a variety of high-speed internet providers available depending on your location. Comcast, Charter, EarthLink, and AT&T are the major players in the world of high-speed internet providers. The two prevalent high-speed technologies are DSL and cable. If you live in a rural or outlying area you may only have one of these technologies available. The average monthly starting rate for either service is about $30 dollars.

The services are typically broken down into packages according to speed. Basic packages allow you to surf the internet, download music, upload photos, and chat with friends. The basic package is sufficient unless you have a specific need. A specific need might be households with several computers, hard-core gamers, streaming HD movies, or if you regularly transfer large files across the internet.

Is Your Phone Smart?

I understand that you may have grown attached to your current phone and it's so "easy to use" and it "does everything you need it to do," but if that phone isn't a smartphone then you are handicapping yourself in a major way. A smartphone is much more than a phone. It's the equivalent of a handheld computer. With a smartphone, the 45 minutes you spend in the waiting room of the doctor's office can be used to take a class, view a webinar, or relax and read a book.

I'm not an advocate of spending money simply to have the latest gadget on the market. You can upgrade without sacrificing your budget. There are several models of smartphones that will fit into your budget. If you prefer the iPhone, there are refurbished models, or you can purchase the model from the previous year. You will have all the features that you need and save some money.

CHAPTER FIVE

GET HELP

I was 20 years old, unloading a 48-foot trailer filled with 55-gallon drums of glue. Sweat streamed from every pore, and there wasn't a dry place on my body. The warehouse manager peers into the trailer then steps inside. He sets his eyes on me, leans against the wall of the trailer and lights a cigarette. He takes a heavy pull on the cigarette, his eyes assessing my every movement, his brain processing and calculating. He releases the imprisoned smoke and casually says, "Son, you won't be successful until you realize that others can do a better job than you by yourself."

In my small world, I figured that if I unloaded the truck by myself I would be demonstrating that I was a hard worker. In reality, businesses make money based on speed and efficiency, which increases output. Increase the output and you increase the revenue. It would have taken me all day to unload that truck. My manager sent over two men that possessed the strength and experience to do the work. We finished unloading the trailer in about an hour.

I never fully practiced that piece of wisdom and, as a result, my entry into entrepreneurship was stressful; I wasted a lot of money and a lot of time. Part of operating a successful business is realizing and accepting some hard truths:

- You don't know everything.

- You can't know everything.

- You don't have time to learn everything.

- Know your limitations and accept them.

- If you are the smartest person in your company then the growth of your company is limited by you.

My first business was a computer repair company. I was extremely good at troubleshooting and repairing computers, and in my euphoric state as a new business owner I figured that was all I needed to know. Repairing computers requires a lot of time, and I was also designing a website for the business, keeping up with my expenses for tax purposes, getting invoices out to customers, ordering parts and learning how to use new software so I could offer my customers additional service options. I was trying to do all of this while holding down a full-time job and maintaining a family. I was overwhelmed, and 24 hours in the day just weren't enough. Working a full-time job, I wasn't able to reply to my customers quickly, and as a result I was starting to lose my repeat customers. I also wasn't nurturing my new customers. I couldn't afford to hire anyone, and I also didn't want to deal with the bureaucracy and legalese that comes along with having an employee. It was becoming apparent to me that I wasn't going to be able to work full-time and have a successful side business if I didn't change some things.

Outsourcing is for You

One evening I'm watching a news show involving a discussion about job outsourcing. I started to think that if so many jobs were being outsourced then I should be able to find an affordable assistant. I spent a few days asking questions and gathering information and decided to enter into the world of the Virtual

Assistant (VA). A VA is generally self-employed and provides professional administrative, technical, or creative (social) assistance to you remotely from a home office. VAs are independent contractors rather than employees so you aren't responsible for any employee-related taxes, insurance or benefits. You also avoid the logistical problem of providing extra office space and purchasing equipment and supplies.

If you were to do a Google search using the words *virtual assistant services* you would be inundated with the names of providers offering services ranging from the pickup of your dry cleaning while you vacation in Hawaii to having a business letter written. There is almost no task that cannot be done if you are willing to pay. You may find that you only need a VA or you may adopt my position. I outsource any task that diverts my focus from generating revenue and customer service.

If you believe that time is money then you should know what your time is worth. I operate multiple side businesses. For each business I assign an hourly value to myself. This helps determine if the time I am spending on a task is making money or losing money. Let's say that I need a web page added to my website. I can add the web page to my website myself, but it would take me approximately three hours and I will probably spend another two hours tweaking the page. I'm not a professional, so the new web page will never have that polished look, and in the end I won't be satisfied. With that said, I charge a rate of $65 an hour for computer repair work. Spending five hours @ $65 to add a page to my website would amount to $325 in lost revenue. I can spend an hour outsourcing this job and have it professionally done with my satisfaction guaranteed for about $75. The remaining four hours can be spent repairing computers or teaching a few free computer classes which always produce two to three new customers. Recognize that your time has a value and place a value on your time.

Managing People

Throughout my years of being in the workplace I had one enduring certainty; I didn't want to be a manager. I didn't have the patience or the desire to manage someone. Part of the allure of becoming an entrepreneur was that I would be my own boss. I would only have to be responsible for myself. This wasn't quite true. I would be my own boss, but I wouldn't just be responsible for myself. I was going to have to manage at least one person other than myself in order to be successful.

It is difficult and it may take some time, but you have to

discard any hang-ups or phobias you may have about managing people, hiring people or the tough task of firing people. Excuses will be given, sob stories told, feelings will be hurt and egos will get bruised, but at the end of the day your decisions are driven by the demands of your business, not by personal feelings.

You need to adopt a managing style. I liken my managing style to that of a coach. I give my VA training, then I let them use their talent and training to get the job done. I monitor their work from a distance and advise as needed. I admonish and give praise accordingly. If I have to micromanage and be deeply involved in the work of the VA, then I will hire a new VA. Keep in mind that your VA will only be as good as the person managing the VA, which is you.

Know What You Need

Working with the first VA I hired reminded me of the experience I have when I go shopping with my wife. My wife and I walk into a store and roam through each department in the store without buying anything, just browsing. Eventually my patience wears thin and I ask her what she is looking for and her answer is always, "I'm not really sure." I know firsthand how frustrating it can be when you're interacting with someone who doesn't know what they want. Don't put your VA in this position. Know as much as possible about the position so you put a qualified person into that position.

I was in the process of starting another business and the county where I resided required some legal documents to go along with my application. I outsourced the work to an attorney. I submitted the documents, and they were rejected. The clerk at the county office said the documents lacked some of the required information. She was correct. The attorney I hired was in general practice and was unaware of the new legal requirements established by my county and state. I should have hired a business attorney. Fortunately, the attorney was ethical and refunded my money. Lesson: know what you need and hire accordingly.

Outsourcing Guidelines

There are several outsourcing websites available but I primarily use odesk.com and elance.com. They are reputable, secure, and fairly easy to use. I have had positive experiences using both websites. Both websites will require you to establish a username and password along with a method of payment, such as a credit or debit card, or you can use a PayPal account. You can also pay by check if you plan on spending at least $500 per week.

Odesk and Elance act as middlemen and are similar to PayPal, but they also serve as matchmakers. They give you direct access to thousands of professionals. You have access to engineers, writers, programmers, website designers, architects, accountants, sales people, voice actors, graphic designers, administrative assistants, video/audio editors and many other professionals. Both sites provide you with sufficient information to help you during the selection process. Bringing the right person onboard isn't done by luck or chance. There are some specific guidelines that, if followed, will produce a pleasant and rewarding experience.

Hours – Only hire individuals with at least 50 hours of work completed. Hiring anyone with less than 50 hours of work is risky. A minimum of 50 hours worked demonstrates that the candidate has the basic skills to adequately perform work in their profession, and it is a good indicator that they will be around if you decide to use them long term.

Stars – Stars are used to grade or rate a candidate. One star is poor and 5 stars are excellent. I stay away from a candidate who isn't in the 4-5 range.

Limitations are Good – Jobs that you create can be billed per

ERIC THOMAS

hour or for a flat fee. Small tasks that can be done in a few hours I will usually list with a flat fee rate. Interested contractors will send you a counter offer if your flat fee rate is too low. I assign long-term jobs an hourly rate, and I will set a limit of 10 hours per week. By limiting the hours I limit my losses. I can see how much work was done in that 10-hour period and determine if the contractor is working productively or wasting hours.

Test Run - For jobs lasting more than 40 hours or if I am looking for a candidate that I want to secure for an ongoing assignment, such as an administrative assistant or bookkeeper, I will take the candidate for a sort of test drive before I fully commit to hiring them. I do this by selecting two to three candidates. I create a small job that consists of a few small tasks that should be completed within two hours. The method used to complete the tasks and the efficiency with which they were completed is used in determining who will be hired for the long-term assignment. The test drive may cost me $20, but it is a small investment in comparison to the time and money I could lose by due to a bad hiring choice.

Avoid the JOAT – When searching for a contractor you will come across those who claim to have skills in every job category. I put these individuals in the JOAT or "jack of all trades" category.

64

During the summer I needed someone to compile a list of contacts at car dealerships that were within a specific ZIP code. I came across a profile of a person who claimed to be skilled as a proofreader, article writer, web designer, video editor, email marketer, voice talent, web researcher and logo designer. I don't know if this person did or didn't have all of these skills, and I wasn't going to make the investment to find out. Ask yourself this question: if you were sick, would you seek a doctor or a doctor/plumber/mechanic/bookkeeper?

Discipline – Managing people doesn't produce income for me so I am always trying to minimize the time spent in this area. I accomplish this by seeking candidates who are disciplined and can work independently. Look for candidates who are involved with or have completed long-term assignments. This is an indication that they can work with minimal supervision.

Set Expectations – During the interview process, communicate clearly to the candidate what you want done. In some situations you may stipulate how you want the job done. You are the employer, but I do caution you against telling a contractor how you want a job done. Insisting that a job be done in a specific manner without your having professional knowledge can endanger the relationship with the contractor and deliver unsatisfactory results.

Milestones and Deadlines – These two terms are often misunderstood, and this misunderstanding produces poor results... and sometimes no results. A milestone is used to gauge progress, and a deadline indicates the completion of the project. The milestone should not be subjective but measureable. A milestone indicating 50% completion of the project might be requiring that six months of bank transactions be put in their proper tax category, 35 sales calls be made or two of four web pages be completed to your satisfaction. The more complex the project, the more milestones you will need. Don't be afraid to set and enforce project milestones.

Recycle – It is easier to rehire than hire. Hiring is a time-consuming process, so I hire with the vision and intention to rehire. I look for candidates who have worked consistently for at least one year. This is an indication that they will be available for rehire when I have more assignments.

Talk Time – Offer and establish a range of times that you expect the contractor to be available to respond to emails and take phone calls. This can be a weekly or daily arrangement. This is especially important when working with contractors overseas where the time zone differences can be substantial.

Pay Market Price – Hiring the least expensive contractor isn't a good practice. When you post a job, contractors will apply with their hourly rate or a price to complete the project. You will notice an average range that many rates from the contractors will fall into. Respect the range and hire within this range. If for some reason you want to experience a contractor who is more or less expensive than the others, then I urge you to really look at the contractor's reviews and rating. A contractor will typically offer a very low rate when trying to get established. On the other end, a contractor with an extensive work history and positive reviews will carry a high rate. I will only use low- or high-rate contractors for specific reasons. I will hire a high-rate contractor for their possession of a rare skill or a low-rate contractor because I am feeling charitable and want to help the contractor get their start.

Don't Make Your Work Personal – My friend Kim operates an online store. She would spend two to three hours a day researching and ordering product to sell in her store. I suggested to her that those two to three hours could be utilized better, so she decided to hire a web researcher to do the work. Kim hired seven different people for the position and none lasted more than two weeks. She kept telling me that "they just aren't getting it." I went to see Kim and in the span of five minutes I understood why all of the contractors she hired weren't "getting it."

Kim didn't like the item numbers used by the vendors on their products so she created descriptions to replace the item numbers. Item number 5983753 became "red stuffed bear with brown nose." Vendors stocked hundreds of "red stuffed bears with brown nose" in various styles and sizes. Removing the item numbers made it impossible for anyone outside of Kim to order product. Don't create systems and shortcuts in your business that only you understand. If only you understand how to operate your business, only you will be operating your business.

Red Flags – Most of the time we receive a warning before the worst happens. Ignoring warning signs from a contractor can cost you money, time and customers. Heed these warning signs.

- Out of touch – No one can be online all the time, though some contractors do make the "always available" claim. A contractor missing your talk time appointments should not be ignored. Establish an expected period where the contractor should be accessible. Consider multiple days without communication to be irregular and sufficient cause to end the contract.

- No connection – There are several countries with areas where the internet service is not reliable. To get hired, a candidate residing in one of these areas will use a friend's stable internet connection to perform the interview. You hire the person and you begin to get excuses like the "power went out" or "the rains came through last week and washed everything away." I understand that things can and do happen, so I allow for that, but on the second major occurrence I end the contract. I will make an exception if there is a good work history with the contractor.

- I need a raise – Contractors who you hire at below-market prices are more likely to ask for a raise soon after they begin work. This is not an issue when you have a small project. You can simply say no. It can be an issue on large projects or long-term assignments where you have placed significant responsibility with the contractor. The last thing you want is for a project or business task to be nearing a deadline and for the contractor to demand a raise. You can reduce the likelihood of this happening by paying market price. You can also implement a bonus system in place of giving raises and, depending on the type of project, you can offer incentive money.

CHAPTER SIX

LEARN THE LANGUAGE

Jeff is a business attorney I met during a PTA meeting. After the meeting we chatted briefly, and I explained that I needed some advice on how to proceed with some ideas. He gave me a business card and told me to visit when I was ready. Several weeks had passed. During that time I had fully developed my ideas, knew what type of help I was going to need and put together a solid toolbox for business. I was ready to bring everything together.

Jeff worked out of a modest but comfortable office. Attorneys bill by the hour so I quickly put forth my ideas. Jeff gave me a lot of positive feedback, but I was struggling to understand some of the terms he was using. Jeff spent more time explaining the business terminology than he did fleshing out my ideas. This is what my mother meant when she would tell me "know before you go." Know the language that isn't common to you before you go see someone. The terminology that Jeff was using was uncommon to me, and it was preventing me from receiving the true benefit of my time with him.

LLC Language

Every business structure has terminology specific to itself, and the LLC is no different. Some of the terms defined here aren't applicable to your business situation, but you should familiarize yourself with the terminology. Know before you go.

Member – A member is a person who owns an interest in an LLC, similar to the stockholder of a corporation. In an LLC the members have the option of running the company themselves or having managers who are or are not members. LLCs can also be created with only one member.

Manager – A manager runs the affairs of an LLC. In most states, an LLC can be either managed by all the members equally, or it can have a manager or managers who may or may not be members.

Managing Member – A managing member is a member of the LLC who runs the operations. If all of the members do not want to manage the LLC, then one or more of them can be designated managing member.

Registered Agent – A registered agent is a person or company you designate to accept official mail and service of process (official notice if your LLC is "served" with a lawsuit) on your behalf. The term "registered agent" is used in most states, but in some states they are referred to as a Statutory Agent, as is the case in Arizona, or a Resident Agent in Maryland. Companies are required to have a Registered Agent, and by law the agent must be available during normal business hours.

Because of this availability requirement I wouldn't advise you to use a friend, employee or yourself as a registered agent. There is no organization monitoring if you have a registered agent, but if a process server or sheriff tries repeatedly to serve legal documents and no one is there to take receipt, the lawsuit process will move forward without you ever knowing about it. This could lead to your state agency that governs LLCs determining that you're not maintaining your registered agent and it will dissolve your company. This can involve you paying re-instatement fees.

It may be unlikely that you get sued, but it is very possible that a discrepancy is found on your taxes and the state can't get in touch with you. The state would proceed to file liens against your assets, and without a registered agent you wouldn't know it happened until it was too late. The bottom line is that there are far too many things that can go wrong by not having a registered agent, and for the cost of getting one it would be foolish not to do so.

Registered agent companies can easily be found by doing a Google search for "registered agent." Freeregisteredagent.com is unique in that they will give you the use of a registered agent in your state for free for one year. Typical fees for the services of a registered agent average around $100.

Organizer – An organizer is responsible for setting up the LLC and filing formation documents with the state agency responsible for registering an LLC - usually the Secretary of State's office. Simply put, an organizer is the person or persons who sign the Articles of Organization. Organizers do not have to be members or owners of the company, nor do they have to be managers of the company. If you hire a company to setup your LLC, then that company is considered the organizer and they will relinquish all powers to the LLC members once the LLC has been formed.

Articles of Organization – The basic document required to create an LLC is called the articles of organization. Some states call it a certificate of formation or certificate of organization. Articles of organization are short, simple documents. In fact, you can usually prepare your own in just a few minutes by filling in the blanks and checking the boxes on a form provided by your state's filing office. Typically, you must provide only your LLC's name, its address, and sometimes the names of all of the owners - called members - but in your case you will be the only member. Generally, all of the LLC owners may prepare and sign the articles, or they can appoint just one person to do so.

Operating Agreement - The operating agreement is the document that establishes the rights and obligations of the members and the rules for running the company. It is the core document that is referred to when issues concerning the LLC and its members need to be resolved. Operating agreements aren't required, but it is a good idea to have one even for a single-member LLC. With an Operating Agreement in place, you separate yourself as an individual from your LLC, even if you are the sole owner (member) of your LLC. Without the formality of an agreement, the LLC can closely resemble a sole proprietorship, which does not limit your personal liability for business debts of the LLC.

Many lenders, such as banks, will request the LLC Operating Agreement to obtain financing. Another reason for an operating agreement is to avoid governance by "default rules." Each state has laws that set out basic operating rules for LLCs and these are called "default rules." By writing an operating agreement, you determine the rules that will govern your LLC's inner workings, rather than having to follow the "default rules" of the state that may or may not be right for your LLC. You do not file the operating agreement with the state. If you send the state your operating agreement it will most likely be discarded.

Annual Report – Most states require you to file a short annual report where you file your articles of organization. This is usually your secretary of state or department of state office. The LLC filing office will send out forms to LLCs each year, and these forms typically require information such as the names and addresses of current LLC members/managers and the name and address of the registered agent and office for service of legal process. Most states require a small fee, which is usually in the $10 to $50 range, but these fees can be higher in a few states.

Initial Report – The initial report, also known as the statement of information, is very similar to a small business annual report. It is by far the lesser known of the two. One of the main reasons for this is that only a handful of states like Alaska, California and Washington (at the time of writing this book) require the report. The initial report typically must be filed between 30-120 days with fees ranging from $20-$100, depending on the state. Information required on the initial report/statement of information generally includes the following:

• The name and address of the registered agent or resident agent.

• The LLC's principal business address; don't worry if this changes, you can update your address in your annual report.

• The names and addresses of the members.

• A description of the business activities being conducted.

Pass-Through – The term Pass-Through isn't unique to the LLC and is one of the features that make the LLC so popular and well suited for the single-owner business. As a single-owner LLC, pass-through means that the profits or losses of the LLC will "pass-through" to you, the owner, who will report the profits or losses on your individual income tax return. You may also hear this referred to as being taxed as a sole proprietor. This simplifies the tax filing process, as the business doesn't have to file a tax return. For all new LLCs, the pass-through income tax status is automatic and is best for you unless you have a specific reason to be taxed as a corporation.

Disregarded Entity - A disregarded entity is a single member LLC that reports its income as a sole proprietorship. This means that your business will not file a tax return. You will report all business income and losses on your personal taxes (Form 1040).

Employer Identification Number (EIN) – Businesses, like individuals, need to be identified uniquely. The employer identification number serves as the unique identifier for businesses just as the social security number is a unique identifier for individuals. The EIN is a federal nine-digit number issued by the Internal Revenue Service (IRS). Sometimes you'll see the EIN referred to as a Tax Identification Number (TIN) or Federal Employer Identification Number (FEIN). The IRS generally requires the following types of businesses to obtain an EIN:

• All corporations

• All Limited Liability Companies (LLCs) with more than one member

• Any business that hires employees, including sole proprietorships and single-member LLCs

As an employee entrepreneur you will in all likelihood be forming a single-member LLC with no employees. In such a case you aren't required to obtain an EIN, but as a general rule it's good for all businesses to have an EIN. You will need the EIN to open business checking accounts and establish accounts with certain vendors. There is no charge for an EIN and the application can be completed online via the IRS website.

CHAPTER SEVEN

COVER YOUR ASSETS

It really doesn't matter what you are doing to generate income outside of your job, but it does matter that you have a business structure in place. Putting your business into a structure allows you to take advantage of the multitude of tax benefits afforded to businesses that aren't available to individuals/employees. Without a business structure all you have is a hobby.

When I started my first business I was overwhelmed when it came to deciding what kind of business structure I was going to implement, and it seemed like the more questions I asked the more confusing it became. Friends and associates that I felt possessed good business acumen all had a different opinion as to which structure I should use. One friend told me that I should remain a sole proprietor. Another friend said I should take on a partner and become a partnership, and a colleague suggested I go the corporation route. I listened to all the suggestions that were being offered. I decided to take an inventory of what I needed for my business and then I would choose a structure that satisfied those needs. With a lot of thought I determined that the business structure I would choose needed to address four primary factors:

- Liability - Protect my assets.

- Recordkeeping - Require little maintenance.

- Taxation - Simplified tax filing.

- Scalable - Grow as my business grows.

Individual and Team

A sole proprietorship is the simplest business structure to start and maintain. Any single-owner business that hasn't filed papers to become an LLC or a corporation is by default a sole proprietorship. A partnership is just as simple a structure as the sole proprietorship and is defined as a single business with more than one owner that has not filed papers to become a corporation or LLC. Both of these structures have one major flaw: neither of them will protect you against liability. Sole proprietors are personally liable for claims against the business. If a sole proprietorship loses a lawsuit or otherwise finds itself in debt, not only will the business be liable for the debt, but the owner/sole proprietor is liable as well. This same characteristic applies to partnerships. Partners are personally liable for all business debts and obligations, including court judgments; so if the business itself can't pay a creditor, such as a supplier, lender, or landlord, the creditor can legally come after any partner's house, car, or other possessions.

Corporation, C or S?

A corporation is legally viewed as an individual entity, separate from its owners, which are called shareholders. This separation is effective in the event the corporation is sued; in such an event shareholders are only liable to the extent of their investments in the corporation. The owners' (shareholders') personal assets are not in jeopardy as they would be if the business was a partnership or sole proprietorship. Any debts that the corporation may acquire are also viewed as the corporation's responsibility. In short, once the business is incorporated, shareholders have the protection of limited liability.

When a business decides to incorporate, it is automatically a C corporation, also called a regular corporation. Because the corporation is considered a separate entity, it is viewed as an individual taxpayer by the IRS, and as a result corporations are subject to double taxation. The income of the corporation is taxed, and the owner (shareholder) also then owes additional taxes on his or her earnings. This is double taxation.

On the other hand you have the S corporation. The S corporation name evolves from Subchapter S of the IRS code, which provides corporations a choice of how they want to be taxed. Once a company is incorporated it can elect S corporation status by filing Form 2553 with the IRS. Under Subchapter S, the corporation's profits and losses are "passed through" the corporation and are reported on the owners' individual tax returns. The corporation itself is not taxed. Small businesses that need the protection of a corporate structure but don't want the double taxation elect the S corporation option.

Corporations provide:

Limited liability for directors, officers, shareholders, and employees.

Enhanced credibility among suppliers and lenders.

Growth potential through the sale of stock.

Certain tax advantages, including tax-deductible business expenses.

Corporations are more complex than other business structures. Due to the costly administrative fees and complex tax and legal requirements, the corporate structure is typically suggested for established, large companies with multiple employees and is not suited for the employee entrepreneur who is starting a business with limited resources.

New Kid on the Block

There have been five traditional business structures: a sole proprietorship, a general partnership, a limited partnership, a C corporation, and an S corporation. Business owners have had to contort their needs into these sometimes limiting structures. In 1977 the state of Wyoming passed the Wyoming LLC Act, and a new structure called the Limited Liability Company (LLC) was introduced in the United States. The Internal Revenue Service (IRS) accepted this new structure, and every state passed laws allowing LLCs. Initially, many state laws required two people to start an LLC, but the law has changed and every state now accepts what is called a one-member LLC. The LLC, in recent years, has become the most popular business structure for small businesses.

The LLC is comprised of the best features of the other business structures. The LLC provides:

Minimal administration - Requires little maintenance.

Limited liability for its owners (Members) - Protected from personal liability for business debts and claims against the LLC.

Taxation - File one tax return.

Scalability - No limit on the number of members. Members may include individuals, corporations, and other LLCs.

Increased credibility - Customers are more likely to view you as a legitimate business.

There are a few business types that generally cannot be LLCs. Banks and insurance companies fall into this category. As an employee entrepreneur you probably aren't planning on starting your own bank or insurance company, but check your state's requirements and the federal tax regulations if you would like more information on what types of companies are restricted from becoming LLCs.

Take an LLC and call me in the morning

The LLC structure isn't a "one size fits all" device, but for businesses in the following situations, the LLC is the perfect elixir.

Startups - LLCs typically work best for startup companies because new businesses often lose money in the first few years. Creating your own LLC will allow you to take those initial business losses and deduct them from other income, like the salary from your full-time job. Let's say you earn a salary of $55,000 from your job and you have $4,000 or more in losses associated with your new business. You can deduct that $4,000 from your income tax, which will reduce your taxable income from $55,000 to $51,000. This will ease the losses of those first few years.

Underinsured - Most startups can't afford to be fully insured. Operating a business underinsured while facing the risk of being sued by customers, suppliers, the public, or your competition is a disaster waiting to happen. If your business is in this position, the best way to protect your personal assets against lawsuits is to form an LLC.

Currently a sole proprietor or general partnership - You may be operating as a sole proprietor or be in a general partnership because these business types are so easily created and managed, but a downturn in business or a small accident can create a big debt situation which can very easily spell the end of your business.

To avoid this situation, why not fill out the LLC articles and file them with your state? Once this is done your personal assets are legally out of reach when it comes to paying off business debts. Your income tax filing status won't change because with an LLC you file your taxes the same as you did when you were a sole proprietor. Converting to an LLC isn't difficult, and it will give you some peace of mind.

Thinking about an S corporation - Starting a business presents a lot of options when it comes to business structures. If you were looking into forming an S corporation, I think you may want to pause and give the LLC some attention. In a lot of ways the LLC was created to be a simplified version of the S corporation. So before you choose an S corporation as your structure, look at the LLC and you will see that it can satisfy the need for an S corporation and do it more efficiently.

You need protection – Milton has a full-time position as a project manager. He develops applications for smartphones as a small side business. One day over lunch he told me that he was making about $70,000 a year from his side business along with the $90,000 salary he earned as a project manager. Milton was operating his side business as a sole proprietor. One day Milton gets an e-mail from someone who purchased his software application stating that the software application corrupted his iPhone. Milton didn't think much about it until he received several more e-mail messages a few days later from other users complaining that his software application corrupted their devices. A few more e-mail messages followed in the coming days, and these carried threats of legal action.

Milton had a family, a home and the side business enabled him to save over $175,000. As a sole proprietor Milton was personally liable. A lawsuit from an unsatisfied customer would probably wipe out his assets and destroy his business. Milton was understandably under a great deal of stress as he asked me for advice. This situation that Milton was facing can happen to any employee entrepreneur that isn't adequately protected. I suggested to Milton that he form an LLC. An LLC would:

- Provide limited liability.

- Limit his liability to the amount he used to start his business, which was $6,000.

• Give him peace of mind.

In the short term, Milton converted from a sole proprietorship to an LLC. In the long term he was able to prove that his software application wasn't the cause of those devices failing and the lawsuit threats disappeared.

CHAPTER EIGHT

WHAT'S IN A NAME

When people find out that you're about to have a child, one of the first questions they ask is "what are you going to name the baby?" Naming a business is in no way as important as naming a child, but I spend a significant amount of time choosing a business name. The thinking behind naming a business and naming a child is similar. You want to make sure that the business name, like the child's name, is a good representation. Choosing a name may be challenging but the suggestions I offer will be beneficial, and the state government agency rules for business names will keep you in compliance. You may not be able to, or want to, incorporate these suggestions, but give them some consideration.

There are potentially complicated and important legal issues that can arise when you choose a business name. I do not get into those potential issues because the scope of those issues is much too large for this chapter and book. I expect that the readers of this book are owners of small businesses that won't generate the millions of dollars in revenue that would inspire concern from a large company about naming infringement.

Don't get personal – A number of small business owners tend to want to name their business after themselves. It's very easy to use your own name as your business name, but it gives the perception that the business is a one-person operation. Bob's Computer Service or Pat's Advertising would work well in a small town where everyone knows Bob or Pat and knows they provide an excellent product or service, but you want your product or service to reach people in far-away places, and your business name needs to express that reach.

Think about tomorrow - Exercise some foresight and consider that your business might expand into other areas. Bob's Computer Service may start out repairing computers but then might move into website design. He has limited himself to a name that only speaks to computer service. An alternative might be Bob's Technical Services.

Be memorable and distinct – Names that include hard-to-pronounce words, abbreviations and acronyms like AGK Plumbing are easily forgotten. Self-titled company names should be avoided as well because they aren't distinct. Here's a good example of memorable and distinctive gone awry. "Dahmer Data Removal" with the tagline "We Eat Your Data" is catchy, memorable and distinct but overwhelmingly offensive and insensitive. You want your name to be memorable without being offensive or negatively provocative. If you didn't know, Jeffrey Dahmer was a serial killer who ate portions of his victims. Enough said.

Easy to spell and pronounce – Incorporate commonly used names and words into your business name and business tagline if you decide to use one.

Availability – The most difficult and maybe the most important naming criteria to adopt is internet availability. Is your business name available as a website (domain name)? Finding a business name that meets the internet availability criteria is a tall order considering there are over 500 million active websites and cybersquatters sitting on thousands of unused domain names. A domain name has to be unique, like a fingerprint. If that domain name is owned by someone, then it's not available to anyone else.

Let's say photography is your hobby and you decide to build it into a side business. You decide on the name Perfect Photos. Without doing a search I will all but guarantee that perfectphotos.com isn't available as a domain name. The words perfect and photo are common words, and common words just aren't available as domain names anymore. If your desired domain name isn't available, get creative. You can play around with phrases like pickaperfectpicture.com or takeaperfectpicture.com.

You may consider using a .net extension instead of the popular .com extension for your domain name. You can go to godaddy.com or another hosting company and find out in seconds if the name is available.

No name can be the same - Two companies operating under the same name in the same state is not allowed. A fairly easy way to determine if the name you picked is being used would be to do a search on the business records portion of the Secretary of State page for your state. You will be able to see any business that has the same name as yours. Another point to remember is that your LLC cannot have the same name as another business that is a C-corporation (i.e., has an "Inc." after its name). So if there's already a "Global Landscaping, Inc." in your state, you can't create Global

Landscaping, LLC.

Don't create confusion - Your LLC name can't be confusingly similar to another business. "Confusingly similar" is typically defined as it being obvious that you're naming your LLC so that the public will confuse your company with a better known company in order that you take some of their business. The two main criteria for confusingly similar names are similarity of name and similar markets.

If you select a name very similar to a direct competitor in the same market, then you are likely to face charges of having a confusingly similar name. If, on the other hand, your name is similar to another company's name, but not identical, and you serve totally different markets, then there probably won't be an issue. When in doubt, pick another name.

The Ending - Each state has slightly different requirements for LLCs, but the general requirement is that your business name must end in one of the following:

- LLC

- L.L.C.

- Limited Liability Company

- Limited Company

Once you've found a legal and available name, you typically don't need to register it with your state. When you file your articles of organization, your business name will automatically be registered.

CHAPTER NINE

FORMING YOUR LLC

Because you are dealing with government agencies, you can expect the process of forming an LLC, the terminology and the requirements for formation to be different in each state. While this can be quite confusing, you have absorbed a wealth of good information that has you ready for formation. This chapter will explain some specific steps in the LLC formation process and will guide you to completion. Unless you have a compelling reason, it's generally best for you to form your LLC in the state in which it will principally be doing business.

Agent – You must have a registered agent. Keep in mind that the registered agent is also known as the statutory agent or the resident agent and may appear as such on the Articles of

Organization, depending on the state in which you are filing. As I previously mentioned, hire a professional Agent. Because of the requirement to be available during normal business hours, don't use yourself or a friend to act on your behalf. Registered agent companies can easily be found by doing a Google search for registered agent. Also, make sure that the registered agent organization you hire has a physical address in the state where you are filing.

Articles - To formally legalize your LLC you must file what is known as the Articles of Organization. In some states the Articles of Organization are called the "certificate of organization" or the "certificate of formation." The Articles of Organization is a simple document that includes information like your business name, address and the names of the members. In most states you file with the Secretary of State office; however, other states may require that you file with a different office such as the State Corporation Commission, Department of Commerce and Consumer Affairs, Department of Consumer and Regulatory Affairs, or the Division of Corporations and Commercial Code.

Your Secretary of State website will provide you with specific information on where to file the Articles of Organization and details concerning your state's filing requirements. Most

Secretaries of State provide fill-in-the-blank PDF templates to file with the State. Here is what you will typically be asked for when filing online:

- Name of the LLC or a valid Name Reservation Number

- Name and address of the person filing for the LLC

- A valid e-mail address

- Mailing Address of the Principal Office of the LLC

- Name and Address of the Registered Agent (must be a physical street address in the state where you are filing, where an individual can be located in-person for the company)

- Name and address of each organizer

- Any optional provisions you need to add to your Articles of Organization

- A major credit card including the 3-digit security code from the signature panel on the back and the expiration date.

Publication requirements – At the writing of this book two states, New York and Arizona, require that the formation of an LLC be made public.

The State of New York - Within 120 days after its articles of organization become effective, the LLC must publish in two newspapers a copy of the articles or a notice related to the formation of the LLC. The newspapers must be designated by the county clerk of the county in which the office of the LLC is located, as stated in the articles of organization. After publication, the printer or publisher of each newspaper will provide you with an affidavit of publication. A Certificate of Publication, with the affidavits of publication of the newspapers attached, must be submitted to the New York Department of State, Division of Corporations. The fee for filing the Certificate of Publication is $50.The Certificate of Publication can be downloaded at www.dos.ny.gov/forms/corps.

The State of Arizona - Within 60 days after the Commission has approved the filing of your LLC's Articles of Organization, you must publish the Articles in a newspaper of general circulation in the Arizona county where it does business for three consecutive publications. The list of acceptable newspapers in each county can be found at www.azcc.gov/divisions/corporations/. Your LLC may be subject to dissolution if you fail to publish. Filing an affidavit of publication is not necessary.

ID Number - After you've filed the Articles to form your LLC, getting your Employee Identification Number (EIN), a.k.a. filing a Form SS-4, is a good next step. Obtaining an EIN only takes a few minutes. You can apply for your EIN online at www.irs.gov, under the Small Businesses & Self Employed section. If you don't want to apply online you can download the form and mail the application, or you can apply over the phone. Applying for your EIN online consists of five steps.

1. Identify the business structure - For you this will be an LLC. Add the number of members in your LLC and select your state.

A page will explain how you are going to be regarded concerning federal taxes. By default you will be classified as a disregarded entity unless you choose otherwise. The IRS will ask why you are requesting an EIN. Select the *starting a new business* option unless one of the other options appeal to your status.

2. Authenticate - Select Individual as the responsible party for your LLC. Add your name and social security number.

3. Addresses - The physical location of your LLC. A P.O. Box address will not be accepted.

4. Details – Legal name of LLC along with its address, start date and 4-5 questions to determine the nature of your business.

5. EIN Confirmation – Determine how you want to receive your EIN confirmation letter.

Your information will be verified and your EIN is immediately issued. Your EIN is eternally attached to that business just as your social security number is eternally attached to you. I strongly suggest you keep the EIN confirmation letter or email in a safe place. If you lose or misplace your EIN you will have to call the IRS, which will give you the number over the phone if you can verify you are an authorized person.

Agreement - Every LLC should have an operating agreement, even single-member LLCs. Having such an agreement can help protect the LLC structure if it's challenged in court. If you have members, then I would consider it foolish not to have an operating agreement. Operating agreements are not complex, but the language is very "governmental," and you want to be sure it is interpreted correctly. You can write your own, but it's much simpler to make use of the many samples available. Lawdepot.com and rocketlawyer.com are sites where you can create an operating agreement online.

You are presented with several questions which are used to gather your information and create the agreement. Upon submission of the form you are given the option to save or print the form. Lawdepot.com and rocketlawyer.com are free if you make use of their trial period; just remember to cancel the subscription before the trial period expires. Remember that your operating agreement does not get filed or submitted with the state. It resides with you to serve as the guiding document for your organization just as the Constitution is the guiding document for the United States. Sign the operating agreement and make a copy. If you have other members they must also sign the agreement and be given a copy. Keep the original copy in a safe place.

Loose Ends

Forming an LLC makes you a legal business on the federal level, but there are a few things that you need to be aware of regarding your state and local government. These may or may not be applicable to your business.

Licenses and Permits (State and Local) – A few states require any business within their borders to get a general business license, but it's more common for a state to require only certain business types to get a license. Businesses that require specialized training, like child care, electricians or food preparation, or businesses that have extensive involvement with consumers, like tax preparation, may need a state license. If a license is required, there will be a fee, and you may be asked to prove you have the necessary training, education or work experience.

Many cities and counties require those doing business within their limits to get a general business license, a.k.a. tax registration. Your city or county government website can help you get one of these. Basically it's an annual license or permit that legally entitles you to operate a business in that locality. I went to the city hall of the city where my business resides and filed a one-page application for a business license. The license fee was based on the estimated revenue of my business, which I conservatively stated as $600 since I was just starting and had no customers.

I also made a visit to my county business office to file my business with the county where I was doing business. In the case of the county, I had to pay a flat fee for the license. Each year I get a notice from the city and county office requesting renewal. Based on the amount of revenue your business generates, you may be exempt from a city or county licensing requirement.

Stay in the zone – Are you "zoned" to work from home? If you're renting, are there any prohibitions on a home-based business? Your business may be home-based, but anything that could increase the landlord's liability (e.g., increased foot traffic in and out of the building) could become problematic. Similarly, if you own a house, are there any zoning ordinances that would prevent your running a home-based business? You can typically avoid any zoning issues if you use some common sense.

If you live in an apartment and your lawn service equipment is consuming multiple parking spaces, then you're going to draw negative attention. Having the agent at the rental office of your apartment complex take delivery of your shipments will also bring some unwanted attention your way. The same applies if you own a home. The neighbors will certainly notify zone enforcement if your yard is cluttered with equipment or if you have storage trailers in your yard. And let's not forget the person who has "sales parties" at their house and the attendees figure it's okay to park in the driveways and yards of the neighbors, or in some cases outright block the neighbors' driveways. All of these behaviors are unacceptable, and they will earn you the unwanted attention of a local government agency. Here is something that I have found to stand true: people generally don't care what you do unless it impacts them negatively, so don't impact them.

Stuff for Sale - If you intend to sell taxable goods or services (online or offline), you will be required to collect state and local sales taxes from your customers. If you sell your products in a state that charges a sales tax or levies a gross receipts or excise tax on businesses, you may have to apply for a tax permit or otherwise register with your state revenue agency.

CHAPTER TEN

LLC HOUSEKEEPING

Depending on your outlook, you may believe the struggle is in the attainment of your desire or in the maintenance of what you have attained. Whether you deem it a struggle or not, maintenance is critical to ensure that your LLC stays in compliance.

Find a home for the money

An LLC must have a bank account. The documents required to open an account will vary by bank. In general, you will need personal identification and your EIN. With online banking being so prevalent there are several options for no/low fee business checking accounts. Credit unions are also good options. If you are established with a local bank then I would start my search there, where personal relationships are still valued. I suggest you use one of the online check printing services available to print your first order of checks. You can save more than a few dollars using online printers. Vistaprint.com is one of the major online printers, and their prices are reasonable.

And the two should never meet

My daughter is in the kitchen as I am rushing to get to a meeting, so I ask her to make me a snack. She grabs a box of raisins and a bag of peanuts. She pours the raisins and peanuts into a bag to create a nice trail mix for me. After lunch I get the bag and notice the peanuts and raisins have been mixed, which isn't my preference. I want the peanuts, so I have to work around the raisins, which is time consuming and tedious.

Now imagine the peanuts are personal transactions and the raisins are business transactions, and you have to separate them. There are hundreds of transactions and it's time to file your taxes. This could make for a very stressful time, but this scenario is easily avoided by not mixing your personal and business finances. It's important to keep your business and personal accounts separate, and making the job of your bookkeeper easier is just one of the benefits.

Business or Hobby

The IRS is sensitive concerning your ability to show that what you are doing is a business and not a hobby. One standard that is used in determining that you are a business and not a hobby is that you have a separate business bank account.

The Look of a Professional

You always want the appearance of professionalism in your business, even if it is a side business. Remember that many successful companies started out as side businesses. Keeping your business finances separate from your personal finances will help enhance your professional image. When you write checks to suppliers or when a customer asks, "Who do I make the check payable to?," they will see the company name on the check and feel that they are doing business with someone who is serious and planning on being around for the long term.

Let's get together

You are not required to hold annual meetings or record meeting minutes for LLCs with multiple members, but holding meetings is an important part of owning an LLC. As a single-member LLC, having a meeting with you as the only participant would be silly, but it's a good habit to keep good records concerning important business decisions. This will serve to further legitimize your status LLC if your status is ever questioned.

LLCs must report

Most states require an LLC to file a short annual report form with the same state office where you filed your Articles of Organization. Your state may call it annual registration, as is the case in Georgia. Most states stipulate that any LLC that does not submit its annual registration is subject to administrative dissolution. In other words, the State will dissolve your LLC. There is a usually a hefty fee, plus past due registration fees, to reinstate an administratively dissolved LLC.

Tax Time

As a single-member LLC your tax returns will be fairly simple. Your LLC won't file any taxes. You will report any profits or losses on your personal tax return. You will report your LLC profits or losses on Schedule C and attach it to your 1040 form.

Sign on the dotted line

To make sure you keep your Limited Liability protection legally in place, you should always sign LLC documents, papers, contracts, agreements and other commitments in the name of the

. LLC, not in your own name. For example:

DiverseMind Publishing, LLC

By: Eric Thomas

Eric Thomas, Member

Failing to sign contracts or other commitments in a way that clearly states that you are acting for the LLC could leave you personally liable for the contract if the LLC can't fulfill the contract. Make this signing procedure a part of your LLC business routine.

State your full name

Any use of the company's name should always include the entire legal name of the company (Diverse Mind Publishing, LLC). This will eliminate any misunderstanding and make it clear to third parties that they are dealing with a limited liability company and not with individual members. All interactions with customers or creditors should be done in the LLC's name, and, if done in writing, on company letterhead. Your company's correspondence, business cards, marketing materials, websites, invoices, statements, tax returns, etc. should use the LLC's full legal name.

Maintain Records

Keep good company records, and keep them in a central location where you can access them immediately. Records needed for tax return purposes, organizational records such as the Company's Articles of Organization, EIN and Operating Agreement, are some of the documents that you should have access to upon request.

Accidents happen

Your LLC provides some liability protections, but you may want some additional protections that are offered by purchasing liability insurance. Most side businesses aren't involved in anything that would warrant liability insurance but look at your situation and accommodate your needs.

APPENDIX A

LLC Operating Agreement

This is a Limited Liability Company Operating Agreement (the "Agreement") made on October 26, 2013. The Members in this agreement are as follows:

Eric Thomas

The Members to this Agreement agree to the following:

<u>Name:</u>

This Limited Liability Company will be known as Diverse Mind Publishing, LLC.

The LLC:

a) The Members have formed a Limited Liability Company.

b) The terms and conditions of their LLC will be outlined in this Agreement.

c) If the Agreement is executed, the LLC Operating Agreement will be in effect on July 02, 2014.

d) The LLC will only be terminated as outlined in this Agreement.

e) The LLC's primary place of business will be 555 Main street, Anytown, Georgia, 00000.

f) The LLC will be governed under the laws of the state of Georgia.

g) The LLC's primary purpose is create training and informational materials for small business.

Contributions:

The Members will make an initial contribution to the LLC as follows:

Eric Thomas: $1,000.00 in Cash

Contributions will be submitted no later than October 26, 2013. All capital contributions are final unless all Members give written consent of withdrawal. All contributions will be deposited into a joint capital account.

Interest:

The Members' ownership interest in the LLC will be as follows:

Eric Thomas: 100%

Costs:

The Members will share costs according to the following percentages:

Eric Thomas: 100%

Profits:

The Members will share the net profits of the LLC according to the following percentages:

Eric Thomas: 100%

- The Members' profit allocation will be accounted by _____ according to the above percentages after the costs of the LLC have been paid or calculated according to the above cost percentages.

- Profit allocations will be distributed 26 times per year.

- Each member must receive 50% of their profit allocation each year from the LLC, although percentages greater than the above listed may be distributed according to a member vote.

- The members are allowed to withdraw from their profit allocation at any time.

- All members will receive enough funds from the LLC to cover their income taxes for total profit allocation by the LLC.

Members and Managers:

- The liability of the Members is limited according to the Limited Liability statutes for the state of Georgia.

- No Member shall be an agent of any other Member by reason of being a Member of the Company.

- All Members of the LLC, by majority vote of Member interest, will maintain 1 Manager(s) to be reelected every year. All Members will vote in each election.

- Members that are not elected as Managers shall not have any control or vote in the operation of the Company's affairs and shall have no power to bind the Company.

- The Managers' authority will be defined by the following unless otherwise stated in the Agreement:

Any decisions requiring a contract or otherwise will require a unanimous vote by all Managers.

Liability of Members and Managers:

All debts, obligations and liabilities of the LLC, whether arising in contract, tort or otherwise, shall be solely the debts, obligations and liabilities of the LLC, and no Member shall be obligated personally for any such debt, obligation or liability of the LLC solely by reason of being a Member. This section does not prevent an LLC Member, should they so choose, from separately agreeing to guaranty or otherwise become liable for a debt which is also of the LLC.

Accounting:

-   All accounts related to the LLC, including contribution and distribution accounts will be audited upon a majority vote of the Members.

-   All Members will maintain a joint contribution account. All Members will maintain a joint distribution account. Members will keep accurate and complete books of account for all accounts related to the LLC. Any Member, whether majority or minority, will be allowed to review all books of account at any time they request.

- Accounting records will be kept on a cash basis.

- All financial records including tax returns and financial statements will be held at the LLC's primary business address and will be accessible to all members.

- The fiscal year will be complete on the last day of December of each year. All Members will present their position on the state of the LLC within two weeks of the completion of each fiscal year.

- The following Members will be able to sign checks from any joint Member account:

    Eric Thomas

New Members:

The LLC will amend this agreement to include new Members upon the written and unanimous vote of all Members.

The name of the LLC may be amended if a new Member is added to the LLC upon the written and unanimous vote of all Members.

Withdrawal or Death:

The Members hereby reserve the right to withdraw from the LLC at any time. Should a Member withdraw from the LLC because of choice or death, the remaining Members will have the option to buy out the remaining shares of the LLC. Should the Members agree to buy out the shares, the shares will be bought in equal amounts by all Members. The Members agree to hire an outside firm to assess the value of the remaining shares. The Members will have 60 days to decide if they want to buy the remaining shares together and disperse them equally. If all Members do not agree to buy the shares, individual Members will then have the right to buy the shares individually. If more than one Member requests to buy the remaining shares, the shares will be split equally among those Members wishing to purchase the shares. If all Members agree by unanimous vote, the LLC may choose to allow a non-Member to buy the shares thereby replacing the previous Member.

If no individual Member(s) finalize a purchase agreement by 30 days, the LLC will be dissolved.

The name of the LLC may be amended upon the written and unanimous vote of all Members if a Member is successfully bought out.

Dissolution:

Should the LLC be dissolved by majority vote or otherwise, the LLC will be liquidated, and the debts will be paid. All remaining funds after debts have been paid will be distributed based on the percentage of ownership interest outlined in this Agreement.

Amendments:

- Amendments may be made hereto upon the unanimous and written consent of all Members.

- Amendments must be expressly written and have the original signatures of all Members.

Settling Disputes:

All Members agree to enter into mediation before filing suit against any other Member or the LLC for any dispute arising from this Agreement or LLC. Members agree to attend one session of mediation before filing suit. If any Member does not attend mediation, or the dispute is not settled after one session of mediation, the Members are free to file suit. Any law suits will be under the jurisdiction of the state of Georgia.

All Members signed hereto agree to the above stated Agreement.

Signed this _____ day of _____, 20____

Signature: _____

Eric Thomas

APPENDIX B

ARTICLES OF ORGANIZATION
OF LIMITED LIABILITY COMPANY

The undersigned organizer hereby adopts the following Articles:

ARTICLE 1

Name

The name of the Limited Liability Company is:

_____

ARTICLE 2

Principal and Mailing Address

2.01 The complete street address of the initial designated principal office is:

_____

_____

_____

2.02 The complete mailing address is:

_____

_____

_____

ARTICLE 3

Registered Agent

3.01 The name of the initial registered agent is:

_____

3.02 The street address of the registered agent is:

_____

_____

_____

ARTICLE 4

Statement of Acceptance by Registered Agent

I, _____, hereby acknowledge that the undersigned individual or corporation accepts the appointment as Initial Registered Agent of _____, the Limited Liability Company which is named in these Articles of Organization.

_____

Registered Agent

ARTICLE 5

Duration

The duration of the Limited Liability Company shall be
_____.

ARTICLE 6

Management

This Limited Liability Company is _____ -
managed.

ARTICLE 7

Members

The members of the Limited Liability Company and their
addresses are named as followed:

_____

_____

_____

_____

_____

_____

_____

_____

_____

ARTICLE 8

Initial Contribution

The total amount of cash and a description of agreed upon value of property other than cash contributed will be:

_____

_____

_____

_____

ARTICLE 9

Purpose

The purpose for which the company is organized is to conduct any and all lawful business for which Limited Liability Companies can be organized pursuant to _____ statute, including but not limited to:

_____

_____

_____.

ARTICLE 10

Liability

Pursuant to _____ statute, any and all debts, obligations or other liabilities of _____ are solely the responsibility of the Limited Liability Company. Any manager or member of _____ is hereby not personally liable for such debts or liabilities solely by reason of their title.

ERIC THOMAS

ARTICLE 11

Organizer

I, _____, residing at _____, execute these Articles of Organization dated this _____ day of _____, 20____.

_____

Organizer

Correspondence information is:

_____

_____

_____

CONNECT WITH ERIC

Thank you so much for joining me on this journey to becoming an entrepreneur.

If you loved the book, **I would really appreciate a short review (even a sentence or two).** I read all the reviews myself and your feedback is vital to making this book better.

You can contact me directly at: Eric@theDiverseMind.com

Follow me on Twitter: @theDiverseMind

Connect with me on Facebook:
www.facebook.com

Thank you again for all your support.

ABOUT ERIC THOMAS

Eric is an entrepreneur, writer, speaker, author and most importantly, a father. For 13 years he has been a successful *Employee Entrepreneur*. Eric currently operates three businesses and is employed by a major corporation as an Instructional Designer and Software Trainer.

OTHER BOOKS BY ERIC THOMAS

The Employee Entrepreneur's Guide to The 5 Mistakes That Can Ruin
Your Business

Made in the USA
San Bernardino, CA
12 August 2018